A JOYFUL JOURNEY

Exploring Your Vibration of Creation

Joyful Journey

MENTORING

Your Path to a Higher Vibration of Creation!

SANDRA KARAS-MALBON
© 2012

Sandra Karas-Malbon

1873 Monterey Drive

Salt Lake City, Utah 84121

801-755-8859

Sandra@JoyfulJourneyMentoring.com

www.JoyfulJourneyMentoring.com

Limits of Liability and Disclaimer of Warranty

The author and publisher shall not be liable for your misuse of this material. This book is strictly for informational and educational purposes.

The purpose of this book is to educate and entertain. The author and/or publisher do not guarantee that anyone following these techniques, suggestions, tips, ideas, or strategies will become successful. The author and/or publisher shall have neither liability nor responsibility to anyone with respect to any loss or damage caused, or alleged to be caused, directly or indirectly by the information contained in this book.

Cover design by Gerald Rogers.

ISBN: 978-0-9848320-0-2

This book is dedicated to my most awesome son, Dustin, whose innate wisdom and compassion from a very young age has amazed me.

CONTENTS

Whatever is True,

Whatever is Noble,

Whatever is Right,

Whatever is Pure,

Whatever is Lovely,

Whatever is Admirable –

If anything is Excellent

or Praiseworthy –

Think on these things.

Philippians 4:8

For as he thinketh in his heart, so is he…

Proverbs 23:7

INTRODUCTION

Be joyful always;

Pray constantly;

Give thanks in all circumstances

1 Thessalonians 5:16-18

If you are anything like me, you may be wondering if the admonishment from the Apostle Paul to the Thessalonians is even possible: How can anyone be joyful *always*, pray constantly, and give thanks in *all* circumstances?

Having experienced chronic and deep depressions since my teen years, I wanted to live a different way; I wanted to be happy. So I set out to discover the feasibility of this scripture. I will share my findings with you in these pages. Furthermore, I had a remarkable "peak experience" that showed me that it is possible to be in the consciousness of joy, prayer, and thanksgiving without ceasing. I'm here to tell you that it is possible, and that your life will never be the same if you choose to take on this challenge of being joyful *always*, praying *constantly*, and giving thanks in absolutely *all* circumstances.

If you complete this challenge, your life will be different in several ways:

- With your joy, you will attract happy people and circumstances into your life.

- You will release drama.

- You will increase your confidence and your intuition to know the right things to do.

- You will feel more deeply your connection to God[1], which will increase your feelings of love and compassion.

- You will have an increase in energy.

- You will have dramatically improved relationships with every*one*, including yourself and your God, and every*thing*, including your money and your resources.

Two thousand years ago, the Apostle Paul wrote instructions in a letter to the Thessalonians (a new community of followers of Jesus) in which he was encouraging them to live by the teachings of Christ by being respectful, living in peace with each other, helping the weak, being patient with everyone, being kind, and not paying back wrong for wrong. These instructions are wise and do-able. Then Paul asked of us the seemingly impossible as quoted above—after all, how can you be joyful when a situation

---

1   There are many names for the Supreme Being / Creator-of-All from worldwide religions, including, among many others: Source, Higher Power, Divine Mind, The Universe, God the Father, Heavenly Father, Lord, Father-Mother God, and Goddess. I am aware that each person reacts to the particular connotation they hold for a word. We may get bogged down in semantics, or we may choose to get the entire message despite the choice of a word. I will be using the word "God" for the Creator-of-All and ask that rather than reacting, you replace my word with your word of choice.

is miserable? How can you be in prayer constantly? And who gives thanks in a thankless circumstance?

The Apostle Paul was an inspirational, hands-on kind of leader! He did not ask of others what he himself was not willing to do. I believe that he knew exactly what he was talking about when he told the Thessalonians to "be joyful always, pray constantly; give thanks in every circumstance." After all, from the Book of Acts, we learn that when Paul was teaching in Philippi, some men took offense and caused Paul to be stripped, severely flogged, and imprisoned. In prison, what did Paul do? Bemoan his fate? Did he ask God why he was being treated so unfairly in the face of doing God's work? No! In a terrible circumstance, he and his partner Silas prayed and sang hymns to God (Acts 16:16-25).

In 2003, I was blessed with a profound "peak experience" that I named "Sitting in the Smile of God." This experience showed me that it is indeed possible to be joyful always.

Sitting in the Smile of God

One morning, like any other, I began my hour-long meditation. I was listening to the sound of rain and, being weary of it, groaned. Then I shifted my thinking. I thought, "The rain is cleansing the air, cleansing the earth, and cleansing my mind. It is a wondrous thing for which I am so grateful."

That shift from complaint to gratitude must have started a domino effect, because next, as I began my prayers for my loved ones, a remarkable thing happened. My heart was filled with a love so deep that I began to extend that love even to people who irritated me—but the irritation was gone! There was no feeling other than that of pure love as I thought of anyone at all, including my personal antagonists (at the time), and, I must admit, particular politicians and certain world leaders whom I would readily disparage. (Yes, I do admit to having had strong opinions, so to feel absolute love and acceptance was highly unusual.)

Words cannot possibly describe the quality of this huge love that I was feeling. It included a "peace that passeth all understanding"[2] and a joy so utterly profound that I felt like I was sitting in a smile as big as my living room—no, as big as my house. No, I felt like I was sitting in the all-encompassing, divine smile of God.

When my meditation time ended, I arose to get ready for the duties of the day, but the feeling did not leave. As I went out onto the road, I found myself loving every driver with whom I shared that road, and praying that they were having an awesome day in every way. There was nothing that any one of them could do that could aggravate me. The love in my heart was so large, there was no room for any emotion less than pure, unconditional love.

Impatience was out of the realm of possibility. At a store, any line, no matter how long, was nothing more than a place for me to be extending divine love to one and all.

And so it went, no matter where I was or whom I encountered. In fact, I was beyond being negatively affected by anyone or any circumstance, and I could see how I was having a positive effect on those around me. There must have been a huge, divine smile on my face, because everyone responded to me with their big smiles. My words to others were of cheer, or compassion, or inspiration.

---

2   Exact quote: "And the peace of God, which passeth all understanding, shall keep your hearts and minds through Christ Jesus" (Philippians 4:7). Because in the midst of turmoil I have been overcome with a profound peace that defies understanding and which I know can only come from Holy Spirit, I resonate with this verse, and paraphrase with all due respect for the full meaning.

This lasted in full effect for an entire two days. On the third day, I could feel a fading, and by the fourth day I was back to "normal," i.e., once again circumstances could sway me emotionally.

My experience of "sitting in the smile of God" produced the kind of ecstasy that we humans seek, and of which we want as much as possible, but it was so beyond the caliber of the highs I have ever found in this world. No thrill or drug-induced experience can compare, I assure you. I speak from quite an array of worldly experience—no angel am I—*any* wonderful feeling of the world that I have ever experienced, from skydiving to lovemaking, cannot come close to the utterly profound joy of *sitting in the smile of God.*

I believe I was given the gift of this experience for a few reasons:

1. I was given to know the contrast between what I don't want (unhappiness) and what I do want (joy!) so that I would do everything in my power to create joy.

2. I was given to know that I have a choice to be happy or unhappy in a given circumstance (I changed my attitude toward the rain from complaining to being in gratitude, which prompted the whole experience).

3. I was given to know who I truly am (and so are YOU!) beneath the layers upon layers of the world's programming. In other words, within us we have the capacity for unbelievably expansive goodness and greatness and pure happiness when we move beyond what "the world" has told us to fear and hate.

4. I am to let you know that we humans are aware of and living only an itty-bitty part of who we truly are, and that right now (not in an "after [earth] life"), we are to follow Jesus by living by his great example, for this will give us an experience *right now* of heaven on earth.

5. I am to share my experience in the hopes that you may be inspired to choose to develop *your* "Christ Consciousness"[3] (as exemplified by Jesus), for this is the primary key to your joyful journey.

Ready to Begin?

I am going to show you HOW to have a joyful journey using the three keys from the Apostle Paul:

Be joyful always;

Pray constantly;

Give thanks in all circumstances

And the verse ends with this line:

…for this is God's will for you in Christ Jesus (1 Thessalonians 5:16-18).

Yes, it is God's Will that we live joyfully always, pray constantly (not sometimes, not only in need, but without ceasing), and to give thanks in all (not some, not the best, but in *all*) circumstances. In other words, God's Will for us is to have an absolutely happy, awesome life *today*! Imagine that! And in "Christ Consciousness" this is possible.

---

3   Jesus lived his life in "Christ Consciousness," that is, he was a vessel for Divine Mind to work through him, as him. "Christ Consciousness" is the state of mind where a human experiences the connection with God as Oneness, knows that he/she is an instrument through which God lives, moves, and has Its being. The Apostle Paul understood that we humans have the same capacity (when we surrender our ego-selves) as Jesus when he said, "Christ in you, your hope of Glory..." (Col. 1:27) and "My old self has been crucified with Christ. It is no longer I who lives, but Christ lives in me" (Galations 2:20).

There are many levels of Truth regarding Jesus' mission here on earth. Throughout this book I will be referring to the most basic levels of his mission, that of Master Teacher, Way-Shower, and the Great Example of "Christ Consciousness." I believe that when we follow him in the most basic ways that he taught and exemplified, that we can actually create heaven on earth right now in our own lives.

CHAPTER 1
Be Joyful Always

The Marriage of Ancient Wisdom and New Science

A number of years ago I learned about and began my practice of some advanced spiritual concepts. Although the concepts are ancient, they are only now in this era being grasped by multitudes of people. We live in a remarkable era wherein the consciousness of human beings has evolved to a point where we understand what the ancient masters have told us all along. Science has evolved to a point where it is proving the existence of God rather than being in opposition for lack of proof. Although we humans have learned the power of Faith, we do appreciate evidence of our beliefs.

One of the ancient masters was the Apostle Paul, who taught: "Be joyful always."

Back in his day approximately 2000 years ago, people must have thought that this admonishment was impossible and simply disregarded the advice. In fact, in this day and age, how many people do *you* know who are "joyful *always*"? Most of us throughout the ages have disregarded this instruction, likely because we've found that circumstances get in the way of our always being in a joyful state of mind. How can one be joyful when one is feeling quite miserable?

There is now scientific evidence that proves *how* it is possible to "be joyful always," and *why it is important* to follow Paul's advice, and I am going to give you simple and effective steps so that you *can* follow Paul's advice, even when circumstances are difficult.

First, let us begin with reviewing the new (relatively speaking) scientific evidence that proves the possibility of being joyful always. This is interesting and fun information.

In the Bible we are told that we were created in the image and likeness of God. Only recently have we understood the full impact of that revelation. The science of quantum physics is showing us that we are like God in that we, too, are creators.

It was discovered that an electron (a component of the atom, of which all matter is comprised) could be either a wave of light or a particle, as determined by the observer. In the initial experiments,[4] scientists were at first baffled because each would see something different from the other. One would see a particle every time he made his observation, and the other scientist would see a wave. It was finally realized that the observer himself would see exactly what he believed he would see, affecting the action of the electron, and inferring that what we believe, we make manifest!

As we now know from science, everything is energy, from our thoughts to the densest of rocks. And our thoughts manage the quality of matter, including our bodies as well as what we experience, which I will show you as we go along. If we believe in illness, guess what we'll create for ourselves? Likewise, if we believe in health, guess what we'll create for ourselves?

---

4 Wave-Particle Duality encountered in *Young's Diffraction Experiment*. Also, on www.YouTube.com, search "Dr. Quantum~Quantum Weirdness" or "The Double Slit Experiment" for excerpts of the explanation provided from the documentary, *What the Bleep Do We Know?*

Universal Laws

Consider also the Laws of the Universe. There are many, they are always in effect, and so it behooves us to know what they are and how they operate so that we may abide by them consciously to our benefit, or otherwise suffer due to unawareness.

- We all know the **Law of Gravity**: What goes up must come down.

  Action: go up.

  Result: will fall down.

  When you climb up a ladder, a tree, or a rock wall, gravity will be pulling at you constantly, without letting up, so you prepare for your ascent to compensate for that downward pull, and you prepare for the descent so that you may control the inevitable landing. This Law is so obvious that compensating for it is instinctive. We don't even think about it; we just do whatever is necessary to work with it so that when we go up, we come down with a soft landing.

There are many Universal Laws, but for our purposes, we will consider how the Law of Cause and Effect, the Law of Attraction, and the Law of Emotion all work together.

As obvious as the Law of Gravity is to us, for some reason, these other Laws seem not so obvious. For example, we don't always recognize the correlation between our actions and our results. Dare I say that this is because we humans often resist being responsible for our actions when we dislike our results? But the Laws are in constant effect, so it's time for us to wake up, see how they are working in our lives, and accept responsibility for our results, so that we may consciously create the results we desire rather than unconsciously creating results we hate.

- We know the **Law of Cause and Effect** (also called Karma, What-goes-around-comes-around, You-reap-what-you-sow): For every action there is a consequence.

Here are some obvious actions and consequences:

Action: plant an acorn.

Result: an oak tree grows.

Action: sow tomato seeds.

Result: reap a harvest of tomatoes.

Here are some seemingly less obvious actions and consequences:

Action: give out anger.

Result: receive anger, lack of cooperation, arguments, and frustration.

Action: send out kindness.

Result: receive kindness, cooperation, and respect.

- Many people in recent years have become aware of the **Law of Attraction**: What you frequently think about, especially with emotion, will be attracted to you, both good and bad.

Thinking: I hate people who are rude and cut in front of me, and dang it, it happens all of the time.

Result: attract people who are rude and cut in front of me all the time.

Feeling: compassion for that person who just cut in front of me, for I don't know what's going on with them that they felt the need to do that.

Result: attract people who have compassion for me when I make a mistake.

If you know that your thinking and feelings are magnetizing to you your next experience, why wouldn't you be very conscientious of the quality of your thoughts and feelings?

- The **Law of Emotion** is about "energy in motion." Emotions are incredibly powerful and will move energy exceedingly quickly. And remember, *everything* is energy.

On the Law of Emotion, Brian Tracy states it succinctly (from his book *Maximum Achievement)*):

The Law of Emotion states that 100 percent of your decisions and subsequent actions are based on emotion. You are not largely emotional, or 90 percent emotional and 10 percent logical, as has been assumed. You are completely emotional. Everything you do is based on an emotion of some kind...

There are only two main categories of emotions: desire and fear. And the things you do, or refrain from doing because of fear, greatly outweigh the number of things you do because of desire...

The more you desire or fear something, the more likely you are to attract it into your life. *A thought without an emotion behind it has no power to influence you one way or the other. An emotion with no thought to guide it causes frustration and unhappiness. But when you have a clear thought, positive or negative, accompanied by an intense emotion of either fear or desire, you activate the various mental laws and begin drawing whatever it is toward you.*

...That is why it is so important for you to keep your thoughts on the things you desire and keep them off the things you fear.

Here are some possible scenarios demonstrating the ripple effect of our emotions:

Emotion: embarrassment because I let that person down and I'm afraid they won't appreciate or trust me anymore.

Result: ignore that person, even blame them, in order to justify my bad feelings so that I can feel good instead (but I don't); attract more embarrassing situations.

Emotion: disappointment because that person let me down; they just don't respect me enough to do it right.

Result: repressed anger at another, and doing the job myself with great resentment; then comes the migraine headache.

Emotion: love—I desire win-win situations for everyone concerned.

Result: respect for another's strengths, forgiveness of errors, and building solid relationships and support of one another.

The Energy Frequency of Thoughts, Emotions, and Things

It's been said that "thoughts are things." As indicated previously, things are actually manifested into physicality by our prevalent thoughts, especially when these thoughts provoke emotion. Thoughts are energy, and material things are denser energy, all vibrating each at its own frequency.

We've heard that "likes attract," and "birds of a feather flock together." It makes sense when we consider how awkward it feels when we are not in company with people at our same level of frequency. We don't feel comfortable with those whom we deem are superior to us in some way, so we judge them as "snooty"; or if we are among people to whom we feel superior, we judge that they "come from the wrong side of the tracks." Really, what it comes down to is that our vibrations are different; we're literally on different frequencies. There is no need for judgments like "snooty" or "beneath us," but only the recognition of the frequencies on which we are operating. We birds of a feather, of a particular frequency, will indeed stick together because that is where we find familiarity, comfort, and pleasure.

I have been asked about the discrepancy in the statements "opposites attract" and "likes attract." Which is it? It is, rather, about prevalent thoughts attracting.

If a person acts from "missing piece syndrome,"[5] i.e., they are looking for someone who has qualities they are missing, that is their prevalent intention and they will therefore attract someone who is opposite, or having the qualities they lack. When a party gal attracts a homebody, likely he's attracted to her vivaciousness and she to his stability. But once they are living together, these qualities often become points of contention. She wants him to go out with her, and he wants her to stay home with him. The reasons for attraction may lose their luster.

On the other hand, people who operate from the higher frequencies of emotions are coming from wholeness. They are therefore not looking for a missing piece to fulfill a lack. Neediness is not the motivation for being with someone. Their prevalent thoughts are to be in partnership with an equal. In this case, people will attract others who are compatible, like-minded.

The chart on Page 40 lists 17 levels of consciousness with their corresponding emotions and the energetic vibration (or frequency) of each emotion. This chart is to assist you in tracking your various emotions throughout the day for a 6-day period.

---

5   Read Shel Silverstein's delightful book, *The Missing Piece Meets the Big O.*

If you are holding anger, you are vibrating at a frequency of 150 microwatts, and you will attract people and situations that are vibrating at the same frequency. If you are embarrassed, you are vibrating at 20 microwatts, and will attract people and situations to you that are vibrating at the same frequency.

As an illustration of how this works, open your left hand, fingers spread and pointing at the same level and toward your right elbow, palm facing toward your belly. Shake this hand slowly. Your left hand represents you vibrating at a low frequency. Now, mirror your right hand to your left, and bring them together, the fingers of right and left interlocking as you slowly shake both hands at the same rate. Your right hand represents another person or situation that is vibrating at the same rate, and how naturally the two interlock together.

Next, keep your left hand in same position, but raise it to shoulder height and shake it more quickly. It represents raising your emotional frequency. Keep your right hand at elbow height, and shaking at the same slower rate as before. Now try to interlock them. Impossible. They are at different heights, therefore, they cannot connect, and even if they were at the same level, the slower vibration simply cannot be interlocked with the faster.

For six days you may track your emotions and notice the correlation with the kind of experiences you have and the people you attract.

The only way to break an undesired pattern is for you to take responsibility for your experience and choose a higher-frequency emotion. Only then will you attract a higher quality of experience.

Example: *My Personal Story*

To illustrate this point, I share with you a recent personal experience in which I started with the emotion of disappointment, allowed myself to steep in it, then attracted a situation in which I permitted anger to dominate, and from there it snowballed until I finally chose to turn it all around.

Recently at the Honolulu airport, in the security line, I was directed to go through the new scanner rather than the metal detector. While in the scanner, I noticed that the other people in my line were not being directed to the scanner. Suddenly, I "saw red." I felt singled out and picked on! My humiliation and anger increased when I was then told that I must also submit to a pat-down, and was asked if I would prefer to do it there, or did I want privacy? Well, I could not imagine the humiliation of being patted down where all could see, so I chose privacy. Two women security guards and I went into a small, hot, stuffy room where one witnessed the other patting me down in my private places. I was now righteously indignant, with anger so intense that my eyes were brimming with tears. I was scheming to take this outrage to the American Civil Liberties Union. Why had I been singled out? Of course they found nothing with which I could terrorize a planeload of people, but I surely wanted to terrorize those airport security people! Vengeance, be mine!

My anger was so strong that I isolated myself for the entire journey home. I did not pray, meditate, be joyful, or give thanks for the stinkin' circumstance. I did not bother to meet and greet my fellow passenger beside whom I sat for six hours. Not one hello from me. I just fumed (when I wasn't distracted by a movie or attempting sleep). What a horrible end to my vacation! But then, I'd been kind of touchy during my vacation when several things didn't go my way, starting with the weather.

17

Yep, when I arrived in Hawaii, there had been a deluge of rain, causing flooding all over the island, including at my son's workplace, where they called everybody back to work to repair the flooded equipment. No employee got to be on vacation, and they all had to spend whatever days were necessary at the plant to fix the flooded equipment, all because of the weather. Which meant that I didn't get to have all of the time I had planned to spend with my son. Bummer.

Then, when I went to rent a car, I discovered that during the Christmas holidays, the cost was exorbitant. I was used to renting a car for $25 a day, and now it was unexpectedly $100 a day! Out of my budget. Those corporate rats, charging "what the market would bear"! Unfair! Bigger bummer!

Furthermore, I was angry at the traffic. Holy moly! I fumed at the development of Oahu without the necessary means of creating infrastructure that could accommodate the growth. I sure was glad not to be living there any more, by golly! Stupid Oahu. Stupid traffic. Grumble, grumble.

Oh, then the rental car got towed away because I was, unknown to me, illegally parked, because there is not adequate parking on that overcrowded island! It cost me $252.53 to retrieve that car! Grrr-umble-grumblty.

Oh, yes, my anger and disappointment were on a roll and did not conclude until I was home again, where I came to my senses and broke the pattern. Finally, I meditated, which is when I find my God-center, experienced "the peace that passeth understanding," and where I discern wisdom and gain insights. This was my Guidance:

My Observant Self: Hmmm. You were rather out of integrity with your beliefs, weren't you? You know: Be Joyful *always*, pray constantly, and give thanks in *all* circumstances. If you had been in integrity at the airport, how would this have gone differently?

My Teachable Self: I would've simply recognized that airport security was doing their jobs, and I just happened to have been selected, as anyone else could've been. I wouldn't have made it a big deal. I could've been neutral.

In fact, even better than neutrality, I could've done the whole situation one better by being a blessing. As soon as my anger arose, instead of cursing, I could've been blessing airport security, blessing the two ladies who may actually be uncomfortable with that part of the job; I could've been blessing all of the travelers there at the airport, blessing all of the airport employees.

Furthermore, I could've been *thankful* for the opportunity that arose from this circumstance, the opportunity to pray for others. I could've been giving thanks to God for the opportunity to raise my consciousness, raise my frequency, and raise the frequency of others.

And had there been any terrorists, with my prayers perhaps I would have influenced a different outcome from the terrorists' intention.

Now in retrospect, I can reframe the whole situation, and raise mine and the two security ladies' vibrations. It is never too late, and this prepares me for the next opportunity to do it right in the moment, as it's happening, rather than in hindsight.

My Observant Self: You are so calm now. How does this feeling of peace compare to last night's anger?

My Teachable Self: Last night was gut-wrenching. My body was as tight and constricted as my mind. I was unfriendly, irritated by both crying children and laughing children, and the passenger next to me who had to disturb me in order to leave her seat. Now, in peace, my body is relaxed, I am understanding of crying children and appreciative of their laughter, and I do not begrudge anyone needing to leave their airplane seat, even though it requires my getting up so they can squeeze by. In fact, I enjoy connecting with others, and my greatest pleasure is in being of assistance. I much prefer the feelings of peace. I choose peace.

(By the way, lest I gave the impression that my entire vacation was a bust, I must assure you that it was not. The majority of my time was happily spent in the wonderful company of family and friends!)

You Are Solely Responsible for How You Feel

There is one thing that will cause you misery. This one thing will keep you from moving forward in any and all areas of your life. This one thing will ensure that you live a life of hell.

This one thing is when you think that happiness will come when someone else will do it your way.

Please stop for a moment, think of your answer[s] to the next statement, and fill in the blank as many times as you have answers:

I will be happy when he / she / it / this situation

....

....

....

I will be happy when he / she / it / this situation

....

....

....

I will be happy when he / she / it / this situation

....

....

....

I will be happy when he / she / it / this situation

....

....

....

If you filled in the blank, this is your cue that you are causing yourself grief. The good news is, upon recognizing this behavior, you can stop and change course.

Can somebody or some situation make you mad or sad or bad?

The answer is no.

It is your *reaction* to what someone does or says (or doesn't do or say) that causes you to feel a particular way.

Many years ago I was in a therapy group of people who experienced a very specific type of childhood trauma. There was one young woman in particular who was demanding that her perpetrator admit the wrongdoing, and demanding that other family members ostracize the alleged perpetrator until the admission was made, or else she would have nothing to do with any of them.

The alleged perpetrator never made the admission, and no family member would ostracize this person. The young woman was miserable and isolated from her family, and her story at every meeting, month after month, was the same. At one meeting, she observed that others in the group were healing and leaving, and wondered at the fact that she had been in the group for the longest, without having a healing.

It was from her that I learned this valuable lesson: she would only be happy if other people met her demands. As long as they wouldn't meet her demands, she was miserable. I figured that she was in for a long haul of misery! Others who healed released their demands upon others, and with or without admissions and apologies, did their own forgiveness work and healed.

So, do you want to be happy and healthy, or do you want to be right? Do you want to be healed, or hold onto your righteous indignation?

Many times we humans have a tendency to think that others need to act first. We justify that we'll forgive after *they* "fess up," because, after all, it was their fault. But in order to raise our frequency, we cannot wait on the actions of others, regardless of whom we deem responsible. We need to be the one to take charge, to act with love first, with or without their apologies. We need to be in charge of managing our own emotions and thoughts and uplifting them to the highest levels regardless of whether or not anyone else does. We will only keep ourselves in lower frequencies where we create more misery for ourselves if we are justifying the reasons why it isn't our fault, and we therefore deserve to blame another.

In my church, at the end of every service, we sing a song called, "Let There Be Peace." The lyrics remind us that: Peace begins with me. Love begins with me. Changing **my** heart opens the space for others to change their hearts. If everybody waited for everybody else to make the first move, nothing would ever get done.

"Let there be peace on earth

And let it begin with *me*..."[6]

The energy of an emotion shifts circumstances. On an invisible level, when sending out love to someone, or a group of people, or an animal, or a situation, the love energy begins to activate a higher-frequency change. We can even change the outcomes of predictions and prophesies! Predictions have been made based on the current set of circumstances with an obvious consequence unless something changes, and we know of prophecies, both ancient and contemporary, that speak of dire end-of-days circumstances on our planet. Both sources of prediction are tools for change, not futures set in stone. If we recognize that we are in the midst of a dire prophesy coming true, it is our wake-up call to change the course away from disaster.

As Children of God, using the Spiritual insight and the power of co-creation available to us, with the Divine unfolding of knowledge of the Universe, we are obligated to raise our consciousness to the level of Christ's and think, feel, and act for the highest good of humanity and our planet.

According to Dr. David Hawkins in his book, *Power vs. Force*, one individual at the level of a 500 frequency (love) counterbalances 750,000 individuals who are below the level of a 200 frequency

---

6   Song by Jill Jackson Miller and Sy Miller written in 1955.

(pride, anger, fear, guilt, shame, etc.). This means *you* can make a difference! Together, in Christ Consciousness, we can make heaven on earth.

CHAPTER 2

The Human Experience

Why?

Let us use our imaginations to follow the macrocosm (God) to the microcosm (you and me) to get an idea of what this life on earth is all about.

As a person who has spent a great deal of time depressed, a question that often arose in my mind was: What is this all about? Why am I here, going through hell? What is the meaning of it all? If it has no meaning, then why not just check out? If it does have meaning, then I want to know what it is!

It has been very important to me to know *Why*.

To explore a possibility of *why*, imagine the Source of All Energy/All Intelligence as a massive light in the middle of a great expanse of nothingness. Source wants to expand Itself, know Itself broadly, wants to create vastly, so it explodes Itself out into every direction.

Imagine as Light is extending out into darkness in every direction, a particular band of rays of energy begin condensing into matter, into what we call the Milky Way Galaxy. Our attention follows the rays, narrowing the scope of our observation to a particular solar system within the galaxy, to where we live. We see the planets in their orbit around our sun.

We now continue to narrow our focus to the third planet from the sun, which we call Earth. We have seen the Source of All Intelligence/All Energy extend Itself out to become suns and planets, and on each planet, Source very likely includes a form of highly intelligent, evolving beings.

On our planet, Source has become all of the elements that we know, from water to soil, from plants to animals. And It wants to know Itself as a creator in the microcosm, so It allows a further individuation of Itself, which becomes what we now call human beings. We are extensions of Source just as our arms, hands, and fingers are extensions of our bodies—not separate, but with different functions from the head or feet or heart or knees. We are in Its likeness in that we are individuated creators, not in the sense of having a similar physical image. After all, Source is *us* in a physical suit appropriate for the earth environment.

Although Source is evolving Itself through all of Its creation throughout the Universe, our focus will be on the human experience on planet Earth.

Please understand that using words to describe concepts is a tricky business, because we speak from how we learned, and our knowledge is growing. Concepts are not static, but expanding. All of the great sages, prophets, and avatars spoke to the people in the language and at the level of understanding of their day. If Jesus were to speak to us today, he would be speaking from the advanced concepts that we now know in this era.

As we incorporate and express our new understandings, we still have a tendency to speak within the old patterns. Because of this, there could appear to be discrepancies, but consider instead that we speak from our various levels of understanding. There is the most basic level of truth, and as our knowledge expands, so does our understanding of another level of truth.

It has been said that we are spiritual beings having a human experience. That is one level of truth. The next level of understanding is that we are Source/God having a human experience.

Source is evolving Itself *through* and *as* us human beings. The same souls (God individuated as us) have lived many incarnations on the planet in order to evolve Its consciousness, from learning how to start fire for warmth in a cave dwelling, to learning how to harness the power of the sun for electricity to warm the apartment dwelling.

When Source individuated, the ego-mind appeared. Ego's purpose is for survival of the species. Ego is aware of danger and will do whatever is necessary to take care. However, humans are evolving out of survival mode, and the transition from ego-domination to higher vibrational living can be chaotic. Old patterns do not change readily at this juncture.

For most of human existence, we have been in ego, or "victim consciousness"[7] because our experience has been of survival. We've had to survive wild, hungry beasts eying us a as a tasty morsel; tribes plundering our villages; greedy land barons, kings, queens, and tyrants; mean employers and conniving ex-spouses; inconsiderate neighbors and invaders and resisters of "the right way"; wars, crusades, and terrorists; accidents and acts of nature leaving us homeless and loved ones lost or dead; unrequited love, abandonment, ridicule; dying from exposure to the sun, or to chemicals, or from smoking, from drinking, or from heartbreak.

---

7   One of the first of four stages of consciousness as identified by Rev. Michael Beckwith in his work, *Life Visioning.*

We have a long history of feeling like the victims of others and of circumstance.

Here is good news: we have evolved to a new level of understanding of how we are the creators of our experience. Up until now, we have not known, or been *conscious of*, our creations. But now that we have learned about quantum physics and the "field of possibility" wherein we create, we know how to create deliberately[8] rather than by the default ("I'm a victim") ego-programming from the ages.

The next level of consciousness from "victim" is to "manifester," which is where we now sit in human evolution.

Our bodies/brains have evolved perfectly according to need. The limbic brain developed for survival, i.e., "fight or flight." But the new brain, or neo-cortex, has developed to assess information rather than being reactionary. Assessing information allows us to move from victimhood into deliberate manifesting, because now we know we have a choice. Now our emotions become a *barometer* of what we are creating.

Refer to the Emotional Vibrations Tracking Chart on Page 40. Here you will see that the emotions of Shame through Pride are indicators of "victim" consciousness. When you track your emotions and find yourself in victimhood, this is simply your cue to raise your vibration into higher frequency emotions. Courage through Love are the higher-frequency emotions from where we may deliberately create from the heart; these indicate "manifester" consciousness.

Joy and Peace indicate "channel" consciousness, which is when

---

8   Find more on "Deliberate Creation" in the Abraham-Hicks materials found at the website www.Abraham-Hicks.com.

your ego-mind surrenders control of your life to Source, which allows God's goodness to channel through you.

Christ Consciousness is indicated when you are permeated with pure joy, when you are infused with a peace that passes all understanding, when you radiate love, peace, and joy that others feel and respond to, and when nothing can perturb you.

So why does this information matter to me? Why does it influence my emotions away from depression? Because I am curious to see what I can create when I am outside of victim consciousness. I am delighted to be part of the work of raising the consciousness of humanity. I am excited to experience the conscious creation of "heaven on earth." I more than anything want to live consciously in Oneness with Source.

The Brain/Body's Design

Knowing the design of the brain/body will help us work with it rather than letting our ignorance of it work against us.

The earthsuit is designed such that every bit of information that you take in follows a very specific path through the brain/body. First, the information comes through one or more of your five senses—from *hearing* a barking dog or a bird's song, to *seeing* dark rain-laden clouds or a rainbow, to *feeling* a kiss or a burned finger, to the *taste* of lemon or honey, to the *scent* of a rose or a chicken farm. That information then travels as electrical signals through the nervous system, up through the brain stem, through the limbic brain where you have an emotional reaction of freeze, flee, or fight to that information, and finally travels a path to the neo-cortex (frontal brain lobes), where rational thought about that information takes place. The information travels this specific path through your body and brain without exception.

Children, who haven't yet developed neural pathways to the neo-cortex where we can reason through a situation, are full-on emotional. We, as children, are little reactors. (And it seems that some of us as we grow never do develop deep neural pathways from the limbic brain to the neo-cortex where we can rationally process our experiences and emotions, so we spend our lives in reaction mode.)

Your Truth and My Truth: Huh?

Our brains also have a filtering system called the "Reticular Activator System" (RAS). If your brain received all of the millions of bits of information that are available at all times, it would blow a fuse. So the RAS protects your brain by allowing through only the bits of information that coincide with your knowledge. Anything outside of your knowledge gets filtered out. It simply does not come to your attention. A common example is that as soon as you buy a particular kind of car of a particular color, you start seeing the same all over the place. Until you made that purchase, you were oblivious to that information. This is why 10 people can witness the same event, but their reports of their observations produce 10 different accounts. Each experiences the event through their own unique filters.

The RAS is very good at its job of protecting our brains from exploding with information, but on the other hand, it also prevents us from seeing all sides to a story. A person who was bitten by a snarling or wildly barking mad dog could very possibly be scared of all dogs, and will react with fear upon encountering one. From their personal experience and therefore knowledge, their RAS is telling them to run away from dogs. A person who has had wonderful experiences with dogs gets a different message from their RAS: dogs are great—and they'll run toward the dog to get a friendly lick!

This is why humans have different reactions to the same things. It is not to say that one is wrong and one is right, for we only know what our experience has taught us. And this is why there is "your truth" and "my truth" and they may not be the same. And as we learned from quantum physics, what we believe and predominantly think about is what we create as our experience.

The Real Truth

If you don't want to be bitten by dogs or have a heart attack whenever you see one, you must realize the truth of the situation. Not all dogs are bad. You simply had a bad experience. You don't have to have another bad experience. In fact, you may create a most lovely experience involving dogs, if you choose. It is in our power of choice that we may change our attitudes, beliefs, and thereby our experiences. And then our RAS expands the information that comes in to include love. Fear may now shrink. Matching the frequency of love, we now attract love-ly experiences into our lives.

Those who desire to experience wisdom, love, understanding, caring, peace, and other high-frequency emotions other than drama, have created neural pathways to the neo-cortex where these states of consciousness are considered and processed. These are the folks who have intuited the higher functioning of the earthsuit and are upgrading the quality of the earth experience.

CHAPTER 3
Tools for Being Joyful Always

As you may surmise from my airport story in Chapter 1, I have not yet achieved the ability *always* to be joyful. However, I've come a long way since my days of frequent and deep depressions that could last for weeks. I am joyful for the majority of my time, and when I slip, I do always reflect on how I made a wrong turn and consider how to correct my course. My feelings of misery are becoming less frequent and more short-lived. I am truly moving in the direction of being "joyful always."

I am going to share with you the tools I use for reflection, making course corrections, and thus creating joy.

First, it is necessary for you to be aware of your feelings at any given time. As stated previously, emotions are most powerful, and you create your life through your thoughts and emotions, for both good and bad.

1. Make a journal for daily writings.

Recording your thoughts, feelings, and behaviors will bring awareness so that you may see the correlations with *how* you are creating your life. (*What* you are creating is self-evident by your every experience, by the very life you are living right now.)

For journaling, I recommend that you get a 1" loose-leaf binder with 8 dividers labeled as follows:

Section 1, "Tracking Emotions": Exercise #2

Section 2, "Gratitude": Exercise #3

Section 3, "Releasing Negative Emotions": Exercise #4

Section 4, "Accomplishments": Exercise #5

Section 5, "Ego Voice Mgmt" Exercise #6

Section 6, "Tracking the Effects of Trash": Exercise #7

Section 7, "Small Vision": Chapter 7

Section 8, "Life Vision": Chapter 8

2. Track Your Emotions.

Use the Emotional Vibrations Tracking Chart[9] on Page 40 to log your emotions for six days. On the day you are tracking, check any of the boxes that correspond to what you are feeling. Track your emotions throughout the entire day. At the end of each day, see which emotions you expressed most frequently.

Record your progress in your journal. Each day, note the correlation between your emotions and who and what experiences you attracted. Do this with neutrality. There is no need for you to berate yourself when your emotions are in the lower frequencies. This is simply about observing so that you may be aware of your creations and make course corrections.

---

9   For further information, read this excellent book: *Power vs. Force: The Hidden Determinants of Human Behavior*, by David R. Hawkins, MD, PhD.

3. Use gratitude to uplift your attitude.

There is nothing better than an attitude of gratitude. It alone can change your life. You cannot have a negative thought when you are thankful. To grow your awareness of all your many blessings, be grateful for everything, large and small. Record your thankfulness in the gratitude section of your notebook daily, and review it often.

For what can you be grateful in the midst of turmoil? Could you be grateful for this very moment in which you have the opportunity to extend love or forgiveness to someone in need?

4. Release your negative emotions.

"Every thought and feeling not born of Spirit is to be rooted up at the proper time so that we may express the truth of our being as children of God." –Mary L. Kupferle

A. *Every day you are to write out negative emotions.* They are inside even the most positive person, and they need to be rooted out, or else they will fester and cause havoc. Addressing the negative emotions within you is not "negative thinking." It is positive to recognize a problem in order to make a course correction.

If you are on a journey and take a wrong turn but you fear "being negative" if you think you are going in the wrong direction, how can you make a course correction?

If you have a sliver in your finger but think that it's negative to look at why there's pain in your finger, how could you ever hope to see the problem and take it out?

Being negative is seeing what is wrong and then just complaining without doing what is required to make it a course correction. Being negative is being blind to the blessing in the problem, and *only* seeing the problem.

Being positive is seeing a problem and going to work on the solution. Being positive is believing in a Truth that is bigger, lighter, lovelier, [w]hol-ier than your current problematic experience, and being willing to move toward that truth until you find yourself living it. Being positive is recognizing the blessing *in the problem*.

B. *Either at the beginning or end of every day, you are to complete whichever of the following statements are appropriate.* (Try them all on, in case you are not aware that one is lurking!) Use a little "i" to keep in mind that it is the fearful ego whose voice you are acknowledging.

i feel fearful because …

i feel angry because …

i feel disgusted because …

i feel frustrated because …

i feel disappointed because …

i feel sad because …

i feel embarrassed because …

i feel guilty because …

i feel _____ because …

C. *Spend several minutes on each one. Write until there is nothing else to write.* You may be surprised at how often there is something to dislodge. With clearings every day, this will open your channels for receiving joy!

D. *Release the negative feelings.* After you have written out these statements, write in big letters with a brightly colored highlighter pen across the page something like this, "God, i release these feelings to You. Take the burden of these lower emotions from me, and bring me into alignment with the highest of vibrations, into Christ Consciousness. I choose to be a conduit of your Goodness. Thank You, God."

E. *Finally, consult with the Emotional Vibrations Tracking Chart (Page 40).* This allows you to compare where you began with where you are after this exercise. Write the statement: "I feel my vibration raising from _____ microwatts to _____ microwatts."

5. List your accomplishments.

List all of your accomplishments, from small to great. Sometimes it's an accomplishment to just get out of bed and brush one's teeth in the morning. Those two things go on the list. For every accomplishment you may be grateful! In fact, when you acknowledge your accomplishments, it causes your brain to start looking for more evidence of your greatness. When your brain starts looking for evidence of all that is right about you—in what ways you are worthy and capable—you raise your energetic frequency and start attracting even more greatness to you. And for that you may be very grateful!

On a daily basis, list your gratitude and accomplishments, and then as you think and write about it, you will come up with many, many more ways in which you are blessed.

6. Manage the little ego voice in your head.

Be aware of the little voice that tells you that you can't, that you're not good enough, that you're tired, weary, inferior, incapable, etc. For every negative statement that you hear in your head, come up with two positive statements that reflect who you are as your Higher Self.

Every day, either in the morning or the evening, you'll be doing Exercise 4, which is writing down the negative statements that come from your little fearful self, using "i." Next, write two statements about the truth of who you are when you live from your Higher Self, using "I". (Example: Voice of ego: i'm too tired to do this today. Voice of Higher self: 1. I will take at least one baby step in the direction of my goal today. 2. I have enough energy to do that.)

7. Keep out the stinky trash.

If you are not living a joyful life, consider what you allow into your head. We are told to be in the world, but not *of* the world. "Do not conform any longer to the pattern of this world, but be transformed by the renewing of your mind. Then you will be able to test and approve what God's will is—his good, pleasing and perfect will." (Rom 12:2, NIV)

Be the gatekeeper of what you allow into your head. A saturation of thoughts and ideas that are "of the world" will not uplift you to the heights where you are destined to experience "joy always."

Pre-plan your entertainment so that when you come home after a long day at work, you have a choice of uplifting, inspiring programming available, rather than succumbing to "the world's programming" out of weariness. By the way, being joyful always will raise your energy level so that you will not experience weariness.

Keep track daily in your journal of how you feel the hours after watching particular programming.

8. Pray constantly.

Dear God, I stand firm in the faith that Your loving law of good is always at work, establishing that which is right and orderly. And so it is.

Figure 1 - *Emotional Vibrations Tracking Chart* *(next page)*

For 6 days, track your emotions throughout the day. Awareness allows you to shift where necessary. At the end of 6 days, if you have chosen to shift into higher states of consciousness, you will attract higher frequency circumstances & people, and thus experience greater joy.

Emotional Vibrations Tracking Chart

Levels of Human Consciousness with Corresponding Emotions & Behaviors	Energy Frequency in Microwatts	Track Your Emotions for 6 Days:					
		1	2	3	4	5	6
Christ Consciousness: whole, enlightened, ineffable	700-1,000						
Peace: bliss, imperturbable	600						
Joy: cheerful, happy, serene, satisfaction, delight, contentment, bliss, optimism, relief, hope, ecstasy, enthusiasm, pleased, gratitude, thanksgiving	540						
Love: reverence, respect, compassion, honor	500						
Reason: understanding, wisdom	400						
Acceptance: forgiveness, harmony, mercy	350						
Willingness: optimism, inspire, hopeful, patient	310						
Neutrality: trust, satisfaction, enabling, release	250						
Courage: affirming, empowering, faith, trust	200						
Pride: scorn, demanding, indifference, inflation, arrogance	175						
Anger: hate, vengeful, antagonistic, aggressive, irate, frustrated, disgusted, annoyed, touchy, perturbed, outraged, upset	150						
Greed: craving, disappointment, enslavement	125						
Fear: anxiety, withdrawal, worry, unsure, nervous, insecure, panicky, threatened, timid	100						
Grief: regret, despondent, depressed, melancholy, gloomy, woeful, sorrowful, alone, heartbroken, distressed, disappointed	75						
Apathy: despair, hopeless, abdication, deferring, indifferent	50						
Guilt: blame, vindictive, destructive, apologetic, sorrowful	30						
Shame: humiliation, despising, embarrassed, unworthy, disgrace, sorrow, remorse, dishonor, disappointment	20						

Information about levels of human consciousness and the frequencies of emotions comes from *Power vs Force: The Hidden Determinants of Human Behavior*, By David R. Hawkins, M.D., Ph.D

Tracking Chart created by Sandra Malbon © 2012.

CHAPTER 4

Pray Constantly

The way to pray is taught by every faith, and I encourage you to use the way you were taught. My purpose here is to have you consider why you should pray without ceasing and increase your knowledge of ways to do so. We will also look at the quality of prayer and at why prayers may or may not be answered.

The Apostle Paul instructed the Thessalonians to "pray constantly." He knew that it is by constant and conscious awareness of our connection to God that we stay righteous, or in other words, in right thinking.

Prayer, you see, is not for the benefit of God. It is for the benefit of humans. It is the means by which we are in communication with our Father, that we know that we are never alone, and that we may be constantly and divinely guided to do what is right, which is His will in all matters.

What Is The Father's Will?

If you are a parent, what do you want for your children? The very best opportunities and outcomes for their highest good? If that is true of an earthly parent, it is so much greater the desire of our God the Father.

The Father's will is that we live in the highest frequencies of emotion; that we experience and extend love. Jesus said that there are only two commandments: "Love God, and love your neighbor as yourself." He also said "Love your enemies" (Matt 5:45) and that your enemy could very well be your neighbor! In other words, Love of *everyone* is the key to the Kingdom.

We are spiritual beings having a human experience. Every single one of us has chosen to have a human experience on Planet Earth. We Spirits are here to explore, experience, and learn. We are here to learn about what happens when we live in the lower frequencies of human consciousness and behavior, and what happens when we live in the higher frequencies. We are here to experience the contrast between those frequencies and to learn that we may make conscious choices about the experiences we want and don't want.

Master teachers have been among us to guide us. They are the ones who have chosen to be clear channels or instruments of God, such as the Apostle Paul. There have been and continue to be many master teachers among us, giving us invaluable instruction. In fact, *you and I* may choose to be clear channels for God's good to pour forth. To be a clear channel or instrument of God requires our praying without ceasing. And this will be easier than you may be imagining!

The very highest levels of consciousness, where we experience the emotions of pure and unadulterated love, joy, and enlightenment, are called "Christ Consciousness." This is where Jesus dwelled continually, never wavering. His connection with God the Father never ceased. This is how Jesus is the Great Example for us.

When we live as Jesus taught us to live, we will be in Christ Consciousness. Jesus said, "Come, follow me...I am the way, the truth, and the life..." (John 14:6). And so we follow him into our very own Christedness.

Praying continually will raise us up to this level. This is the Father's Will for us.

Prayer—Answered and Unanswered

"Ask, and it will be given to you; seek, and you will find; knock, and the door will be opened to you. For everyone who asks, receives; he who seeks, finds; and to him who knocks, the door will be opened." Matt 7:7

With Jesus' promise, why does it feel like sometimes prayers go unanswered?

Let's explore some reasons.

Consider the quality of a prayer. Prayers that ask for "our side to win" cannot be answered by God. If both teams have the same prayer, and assuming all things being equal, how could God take sides? The side that wins will think that their prayer was answered and the other side will wonder why theirs was not.

Whatever the outcome for your side, this kind of prayer is answered by *you,* according to your willingness, skill, and effort; but God the Father will not take sides on behalf of one Child over another. Would you as a loving and fair-minded parent take the side of one of your children over another? You may reward high-frequency *behavior* over low, which by Law, in and of itself, will bring reward. But would you stack odds against another child so that he/she would lose? If you wouldn't, how could we ever expect God our Father to do so?

The prayer that *can* be answered by God is the one that asks that we do our best, have strength, courage, a sense of fair play, that we demonstrate excellent skill, and that our strategies are top-notch and that we are open to hearing Divine Guidance. Our edge is greater when we are receptive to hearing Divine Guidance. Guidance is given to one and all without exception, but who is more open to hearing and following? The one who prays to be receptive to the Guidance.

A prayer may seem to go unanswered because we do not recognize the answer. An example is illustrated with this classic story:

A man was sitting on his front porch during a flood, and the water was up to the porch. As the man prayed for God to save him from the flood, a neighbor rowing to higher ground told the man to hop in the boat. The man on the porch replied, "No thank you! I have faith that God is going to save me!" With that, the man in the boat rowed away.

The water kept rising and while the man was standing on his roof, praying for God to save him, a sheriff's boat came by. The deputy yelled for the man to hop into his boat, and he would take him to higher ground. The man on the roof replied, "No thank you! I have faith that God is going to save me!" With that, the sheriff's deputy in the boat sped away to search for others who needed rescuing.

The man was now standing on top of his chimney, the floodwaters were up to his knees, and he was praying fervently for God to rescue him. A helicopter spotted the man standing in the water on top of his chimney, and flew down. The pilot yelled at him to grab on to the helicopter and he would take him to higher ground. The man, again, replied, "No thank you! I have faith that God is going to save me!" The helicopter pilot then sped away looking for others who would be willing to be rescued.

The man drowned in the flood and was standing before God. God was looking at the man, shrugging His shoulders with His hands held out wide. With a perplexed look on His face, God saying, "Why are you here?" The man replied, "I had faith that you would rescue me, and you didn't." God replied with frustration, "I sent two boats and a helicopter, what more did you want?"

How do we ensure that we are not blind, but open to seeing the answer?

- We must recognize that God works through people. People are very often the conduit / instrument through which God provides the answer.

- God gives us Divine Ideas. We know it's a Divine Idea by its quality. It is a Divine Idea if it flows into being effortlessly, is of high frequency (check the chart!), is a win-win for all concerned, and gives you a "peace that passes understanding."

- Often it is during quiet time that the answer flows in. After prayer—the asking part of communication with God—comes meditation—the quiet listening part of communication. Do you have a two-part practice?

- Another reason that our prayers may seem to go unanswered is our own default programming that causes blocks to our goodness coming in. We need to be aware of these blocks and remove them.

I love this age of computers because the operation and language of computers is a perfect metaphor for our lives. Just as a computer is programmed, so are we—by parents, society, our culture and subcultures, teachers, our own childhood misunderstandings, and our survival mechanisms. As with a computer that has default settings in the programming, so do we. We can change a setting, for example, from font Times New Roman size 12 to Ariel size 10, but the change will always return to the default when we begin a new document unless we make a permanent change in the system. So it is with humans. We may change our program from being overweight to being at target weight, but we will return to the default programming of overweight unless we make a permanent change in the system.

It is the negative programming that blocks our channels from receiving God's ever-flowing goodness. God pours blessings into everybody's lives at all times. Jesus said "[God] causes his sun to rise on the evil and the good, and sends rain on the righteous and the unrighteous" (Matt 5:45). The more we live in high-frequency consciousness, the more we will be unblocked and open to receive.

I am going to further break this down into a graphic image of how it works.

Imagine a picture of yourself as a Child of God with many rays of light coming from God/Source and entering at your head. You are immersed in a rainbow of light that is penetrating your very physical being; however, you notice that in some areas the rays of light are flooding and in some areas just trickling. Each of those rays of light represents a blessing from God/Source. There is health, prosperity, love, wisdom, worthiness, faith, courage, strength, intelligence, knowledge, joy, discernment, compassion—you name it. However, your programming has created plugs in some of the rays. For example, if you were programmed as a child that illness served you, then there is a block in the health ray. It may be a huge plug or a small plug, but that is keeping you from receiving your full measure of Health. No matter how much you pray, if your programming for illness serves you (in getting attention and sympathy, for example), then that block will not be dissolved.

God is always sending His blessings, they pour forth constantly, but your programming may be getting in the way. With this awareness, you can get out of your and God's way with a prayer of willingness to change course. Willingness is a fulcrum point in the levels of human consciousness. It's at a powerful frequency of 300 that can counterbalance 90,000 individuals who are operating at lower frequencies. But most importantly, it has the power to turn the tide for you.

Ways to Pray Constantly

A master teacher, St. Francis of Assisi, gave an example of a high-frequency prayer that asks for the best for one and all. This is a perfect prayer to carry in your heart at all times, a prayer to use continually:

Lord, make me an instrument of your peace.

Where there is hatred, let me sow love.

Where there is injury, pardon.

Where there is doubt, faith.

Where there is despair, hope.

Where there is darkness, light.

Where there is sadness, joy.

O Divine Master,

Grant that I may not so much seek to be consoled, as to console;

To be understood, as to understand;

To be loved, as to love.

For it is in giving that we receive.

It is in pardoning that we are pardoned,

And it is in dying that we are born to Eternal Life.

Amen.

"Making a joyful noise unto the Lord." Sing! Hymns, praises to the Lord, your affirmations, contemporary songs with uplifting lyrics—what a delightful way to pray constantly. Sing everywhere—in the shower, of course; in the car with windows up or down; while riding your bike, taking a walk, cooking a meal, washing the dishes…and don't be concerned with the quality of your voice. This is between you and God, and God loves your voice.

Asking to be of service is what I pray every morning: "God, where will You have me go today, who will You have me meet, and what will You have me say or do?" This prayer may involve me in serving unexpectedly as a spiritual counselor, or maybe just a good friend with a listening ear. I may be guided to make a phone call or to send a letter, card, e-mail to someone, expressing words of inspiration or letting them know I care. I may be asked to pray for a driver who has just cut me off.

Expressing gratitude to God for all things, large and small, is a wonderful way to pray without ceasing. I even give thanks for experiences that push me to the edge and result in personal growth. I can't tell you the number of times that I pray, "Thank you God that I am late so that I may learn about patience as I drive calmly, within the speed limit, and with love for whomever the slow driver is in front of me." Or "Thank you God for this big scary opportunity to *stretch*. I am your instrument. It is not I, but You the Father who does this work though me!" Or, "I am so grateful for this snowy day so that I will work productively rather than being tempted to go play." Or, "Thank you for my little buddy, Tiddles, who curls up with me every morning during my inspirational reading and purrs while I read."

In my gratitude book I have listed: the hot-water shower that comes into my bathroom in copious amounts with the turn of a handle; clean water that comes from the kitchen spigot; a handy vacuum that sucks up generous amounts of cat hair. Oh, did I mention my children, my grandchildren, my sisters and brother, nieces and nephews, and friends? Quality time spent with my parents and grandparents and my husband before they all passed away? I'm grateful for teachers and leaders and lessons and creativity, and for my talents and skills. I have a very long list, of which this is a small sampling.

Now, make your list in the gratitude section of your journal.

Asking for a blessing for anyone who irritates you is a perfect way to "love your enemy." And, in case you forget to do it in the midst of your irritation, it is never too late to later reframe it, for that will still change the energy of the incident and the people involved to a higher frequency.

I'll share a personal story about the first time I did exactly this. I was driving home from *A Course In Miracles* study group. The big concept in *ACIM* is that our only purpose is to extend God's Love, and that we are either extending Love, or we are asking for Love. People who are behaving badly are really only asking for Love. I loved that evening's lesson and was in a great mood, at a high vibrational level. I was driving home on a 6-line highway with 3 lanes in each direction. I was in the middle south-bound lane. Traffic was light at 9:00 pm.

Ahead in my lane was a car going more slowly than I, so I moved to the left to pass. He moved to the left as well, remaining at the same slower speed. So I moved to the right. So did he. Now I was irritated that someone was playing a game. And no one, but no one, gets the best of me! So I hit the accelerator and sped around him to the left, keeping my speed up to ensure that he couldn't get in front of me again, and up ahead the traffic light was turning red! I had to screech to a halt, as he pulled up right next to me. Was my face red, or what?

The light turned green, and he stepped on the gas and changed lanes in front of me. Now I was wondering what I did to create this karma? I don't do this sort of thing! And I was just coming from a spiritual study group, for goodness sakes. What could this be about? I was thinking this as I once again stepped on the gas, overtook him, and left him in the dust.

But being introspective, at home I meditated on the whole incident. What I realized is that I may not play games like that on the road, but I do get irritated with slow drivers and hate being behind one. So I attracted someone who would push those buttons. As long as I have triggers, I will be triggered. If I didn't have a hot button, then that driver's behavior wouldn't have bothered me. As simple as that.

But furthermore, I missed my opportunity to extend Love to someone who was asking for it. I got so caught up in my pattern of needing to not be obstructed on the road, that even coming from *ACIM* group where we had been discussing how to extend Love, I didn't in the moment see the higher truth that was at play.

So, in retrospect I asked God to bless that driver, bless me that I would remember that I'm an instrument through which God may do His work, and help me see that *every* situation is an opportunity to be that instrument.

Being in prayer constantly will make it easy to "give thanks in all circumstances."

CHAPTER 5

Give Thanks in All Circumstances

To give thanks in *all* circumstances is certainly a leap of faith. How does one give thanks in a *thankless* circumstance?

To give thanks while in the midst of a problem will require your faith in knowing that God makes good of any and all situations, knowing that all is in Divine Order, and knowing that "this is here to bless me" or "I'm here to be a blessing."

Another way of looking at a challenging circumstance is to know that "this, too, shall pass." When you reflect on your life, don't you see a series of good-bad-good-bad-good situations? So it is with the human experience. In turmoil, we must keep this in mind: this, too, shall pass.

A case in point is the familiar Bible story of Joseph, favorite son of Jacob. This story, summarized here, illustrates how Joseph was of good cheer in every situation (except perhaps when he was thrown into the pit by his brothers!) and how God made good of every situation, either blessing Joseph or making *him* a blessing to others. We also find the good-bad-good-bad-good scenario, where this, too, does pass.

Joseph Sold into Slavery

Joseph was sold by his jealous brothers to merchants on their way to Egypt, where the merchants in turn sold him into slavery. In Egypt Joseph was sold to Potiphar, a wealthy, upright, well-respected man who appreciated Joseph. But then, so did Potiphar's wife appreciate Joseph, and when he wouldn't respond to her advances, she in retaliation accused him of wrongdoing towards her. Surprised and angry at Joseph's alleged betrayal, Potiphar had Joseph imprisoned. Here, Joseph's unmitigated cheerful nature caught the eye of the keeper of the prison, who made life easy for him. It so happened that two of Pharaoh's servants were in prison at this time, and when each had dreams, Joseph was able to interpret both. One of the servants was released from prison, and resumed his place with the Pharaoh. When the Pharaoh himself had a dream that needed interpretation, the servant remembered Joseph. Joseph not only interpreted the dream, but he also advised Pharaoh of a solution to the prophesied event, with which Pharaoh was impressed, putting Joseph in charge of the plan and making him governor of the land.

During the prophesied period of famine, Joseph's brothers came to Egypt to buy grain. It was Joseph, governor of the land, with whom they had to meet to negotiate a purchase. At a second reunion, Joseph told his brothers, "You intended to harm me, but God intended it for good to accomplish what is now being done, the saving of many lives."

Another example of the bad-good-bad-good theme, and that blessings come from every circumstance, is one of my favorite stories from the Zen Buddhist tradition.

The Wise Farmer

One day, a farmer's horse runs away. All of the villagers react with sympathy, saying, "Oh that is so bad."

The farmer merely says, "Maybe yes, maybe no."

The next day the horse returns, followed by a whole herd of wild horses. The farmer and his son corral the herd. Astonished, the villagers react, saying "Oh, this is so very good."

The farmer merely says, "Maybe yes, maybe no."

While the farmer's son is taming one of the horses, he falls and breaks his leg. Now the farmer has no one to help him on the farm while his son is laid up in bed with his broken leg.

All of the villagers react with sympathy, "Oh that is so bad."

The farmer merely says, "Maybe yes, maybe no."

The next day the King's army rides through the village, taking all of the young men to war with them. Of course, guess who had a broken leg and couldn't go?

Ah, so....it's all good.

Corrie Ten Boom Gives Thanks for Fleas

In Corrie ten Boom's autobiography, *The Hiding Place*, she tells of when she and her sister Betsy were taken to the extermination camp, Ravensbrück. The ten Boom family, although Christian, were hauled off to the camps because they were caught hiding Jews in their home during Hitler's Nazi regime. Upon their arrival at Ravensbrück, a number of women were stripped of all personal effects and their clothing, were given thin cotton dresses to wear instead, and were ushered through a line where they were patted down for Nazi-designated "contraband" on their way to the barracks.

Under that thin cotton dress, Corrie managed to hide her prized possessions—a Bible and a bottle of vitamins for her ailing sister. Her contraband was quite visible with its bulk, but she prayed for its safe passage. She writes, "The woman in front of me was searched three times. Behind me, Betsy was searched. No hand touched me."

Her description of Barracks 28 is heart-wrenching. Corrie writes: "...The vast room was in semi-twilight. Our noses told us, first, that the place was filthy: somewhere plumbing had backed up, the bedding was soiled and rancid..." They later learned that the building had been designed to hold 400, but 1400 women were crammed into the space. "Eight acrid and overflowing toilets served the entire room."

"...we saw that [our beds] were great square piers stacked three high, and wedged side by side and end to end with only an occasional narrow aisle slicing through." She further described their having to "haul" themselves up to the second level of this stack, and crawling (as a third tier was stacked above) across three other straw-covered platforms to reach where she and Betsy were assigned to sleep. The "mattress" was straw reeking of urine and vomit. And, they discovered, fleas!

In dismay, Betsy prayed, "Show us. Show us," then said to Corrie, "He's given us the answer!...in First Thessalonians.... give thanks in all circumstances, for this is the will of God in Jesus Christ. That's what we can do. We can start right now to thank God for every single thing about this new barracks!"

Corrie and Betsy then began to give thanks, right there in the middle of that situation. Corrie writes, "I looked down at the

Bible. 'Yes! Thank You, dear Lord, that there was no inspection when we entered here! Thank You for all the women, here in this room, who will meet You in these pages.' Betsy said 'Yes, thank You for the very crowding here. Since we're packed so close, that many more will hear!'" Betsy continues, "Thank You for the fleas." At which point Corrie protests and Betsy responds, "Give thanks in *all* circumstances…it doesn't say in pleasant circumstances. Fleas are part of this place where God has put us."

Corrie continues her story, describing how she and Betsy set up a covert Bible study in the far corner of the barracks, where they sang hymns and read scripture. It becomes so popular that they schedule a second Bible study group to follow the first. The big mystery was how were they managing to get away with this "unacceptable" activity? We finally learn the answer—no security guard would come near that flea-infested barracks.

Corrie writes, "As the rest of the world grew stranger, one thing became increasingly clear. And that was the reason the two of us were here. Why others should suffer we were not shown. As for us…our Bible was the center of an ever-widening circle of help and hope…The blacker the night around us grew, the brighter and truer and more beautiful burned the word of God."

Shawn's Story

Of course, I have my own story to tell. This is a bad-good-bad-good story of many blessings within the context of dying.

In late 2003, my husband was laid off from his job. A worrier, Shawn became exceedingly distressed. Very bad. At one point, when he was exhausted from worry, he finally heard my words to have faith that there was something better for him in store, and he "let go and let God." He released his burdens, lightened up, and found peace of mind—yes, that "peace that passeth understanding." With that came the turnaround. He started getting calls from all over the country from people in his industry who had heard that he was available for consultancy work. So much work flowed to him in 2004 that he had to start turning it away. His consultancy fees exceeded his former salary. And he got to learn of the value and respect that others held for him in his industry. What a blessing for him. Very good.

At the end of 2004, he was offered a position in Australia. We went to Queensland, where we spent time in Brisbane and were met by a company hospitality husband-and-wife team (thank you, Lynnie and Noelie) in the small coastal city of Mackay, where our royal-treatment tour began. We then went to Eungella National Park in the outback where we would live in Moranbah if Shawn accepted the position. Anticipating a new adventure, we accepted, although there was some trepidation at leaving our children and new grandchildren for a distant land. Good and bad.

In preparation for our move, Shawn was required to have a full medical exam. He did fine, but did not come any where near passing the spirometry test. Red flag indicating something bad.

Meanwhile, a company in the city where we lived offered Shawn a position when they heard that he was leaving for Australia. They had used his consultancy services and so valued him that they negotiated a very fine employment package to entice us away from going Down Under. We decided to forego the Aussie adventure to stay closer to our families. Even though Shawn did well with his own business, he preferred the security and discipline of employment, so for him this was a blessing. Goodness, goodness.

Shawn developed a cough that for weeks would not go away. He went to the doctor, an x-ray was taken of his lungs, and the malignant tumor was discovered in July of 2005. Bad.

Small cell lung cancer is aggressive, and had we been in the Aussie outback, he would not have gotten the immediate and exhaustive medical attention he needed to extend his life. He could have been dead within weeks. A blessing that we did not go.

The prognosis for small cell lung cancer is very poor, so Shawn knew from the beginning that he was living on borrowed time. An agnostic, he began to consider the possibility of a power greater than himself. A sarcastic Brit, his tone began to change as he gladly accepted all prayers, of which there were many. He hung up a picture of Jesus over his desk. Good.

One Sunday morning as I was preparing to leave for a very special service at my church, he called out in alarm for me to look at his fingers. The tips of three of the fingers on his right hand were dark purple. Instead of church, off we went to the ER. (Bad!) We were there all day, admitted to the hospital finally that night, and they ran tests until they found what was wrong. Turned out blood clots had gone to his fingertips and lodged there. They discovered that the clots had made it to the fingertips through a hole in his heart that he didn't even know he had, rather than making their way to his lungs or brain to cause an aneurism. More blessing, because he knew that he had things to finish before he left this earth, and he'd better take care of it sooner rather than later. Good.

He moved into action. We went to England for his final visit with his family. His daughter moved her wedding date up by many months to ensure that he could walk her down aisle. He visited an estate planning attorney to make his living trust and will. He put all his business in order and then told me that he could die in peace because he had accomplished all that he had set out to do, primarily making sure his family was well taken care of.

And then he lightened up. He was an inspiration to everyone he met, he was so at peace with his dying. He even found humor in incidents that at the time scared him, like the day all of his hair fell out as a result of the chemo treatments. He and his new friends at the oncologist's office shared stories during their hours-long chemo treatments together. A fellow chemo patient had been driving his car with the window open one day. When he got home, he discovered to his surprise that he was bald. When he looked in the backseat of his car, he found that all of his hair had blown out into the backseat. As for Shawn, he and our long-haired cat were vying for who could shed the most hair; then one day, Shawn found that he could grab it out by the fistful. After he cried (his thick, dark hair was one of his nicest assets for a man approaching 60), he laughed.

In his job, where he had been employed for only a few months before the cancer was discovered, he found that he could work fewer and fewer hours. Furthermore, after a year of treatment he was found to be in remission but was told that recurrence was highly likely and that it would metastasize in the brain. He had an option to have his brain radiated as a preventive measure, with the side effect of short-term memory loss. Due diligence showed that it was absolutely an individual matter, each person having their own reactions to this treatment, and only after the fact. Being clueless as to what the pros and cons were of doing or not doing this treatment, he chose the radiation. Afterwards he regretted it, as he said that it affected his ability to do his work. He would proof his worksheets and find mistakes, which worried him to no end. Finally, without the clear thinking that he deemed necessary to serve his clients well, he arranged to go on medical leave. Bad, in his opinion.

Now, here's the last blessing that came from bad: had he been at the company that had laid him off in 2003, he would not have had the support (opinion based on knowledge of that company) I'm about to share. And had we been in Australia, I'm sure cancer would have taken him soon after our arrival. But even though his employment was less than a year, in this new company the powers-that-be had the compassion to go against company regulations and allowed an extensive paid medical leave. Further, they kept his medical insurance in full effect, and even though he did not qualify by length of employment with them, they put in effect a life insurance policy, from which I benefitted when Shawn passed away in 2007. What this all means is that we were not left destitute from medical bills and the sudden loss of income, a relief for both Shawn and for me.

Although Shawn was not a prayerful man, he was a thankful man during the process of his dying.

And although I miss Shawn, during deep meditations I have had "visits" from him, assuring me that he is alive and well and happier than he ever was while in this lifetime on earth. I am thankful for his sharing from "the other side."

Tracking Your Blessings

1. In your journal Section 1, "Tracking Emotions," track your emotions during a particular circumstance that seems bad at the time.

2. Expect that "this, too, will pass," and keep your eyes open for the blessing. Record in Section 4, "Accomplishments," how you were blessed, or how you were the blessing. Review your journal often.

CHAPTER 6

For This Is God's Will For You in Christ Jesus

We humans are funny creatures, I've noticed. When we are between a rock and a hard place and don't know what the heck to do, we seem to be far more receptive to knowing God's will for us. We beseech God to show us what to do, for seemingly it is beyond us to know.

Yet when we are in a cycle of things going just fine and someone brings up the subject of God's will, suddenly we fear God's will, that it might be opposed to our will of current good fortune. If things are going fine (interpret: *my way*) we fear that God may not want us to have what we have, that He may want us to have tribulation from which we may learn and grow, that He may want us to live a solemn life rather than a fun one.

Have you noticed that about yourself?

List here what you may fear as God's will for you that you do not want:

....

....

....

As Paul told the Thessalonians (and I paraphrase), God's will for you is to be joyful always, to be connected to Him through constant communication (prayer), and to have a thankful heart with the belief that no matter what, God's love and grace will bring you an outcome of good beyond your expectations.

In Chapter 12 of the book of Luke, beginning with verse 22, Jesus is telling his disciples not to worry about what to eat, or wear, or about the body at all, for the Father knows our needs and provides everything. It is done in nature, so why would humans not have the same loving attention from our Father? When we seek first the Kingdom, all else will be also given. Jesus said, "It is the Father's good pleasure to give you the keys to the Kingdom."

What *is* this Kingdom we are to seek as God wills for us?

- As described in I Thessalonians 5: 16-18 and in Luke 12, and as shown by Jesus' healings, it is nothing short of the most joyful, richly blessed, abundant, healthy, loving life possible.

- It is Christ Consciousness that we attain as we live as Jesus showed us. In the simplest terms of today's advanced understanding, it is about living in the highest microwatt frequencies of human consciousness—that is, with courage, willingness, acceptance, love, joy, peace, and enlightenment (refer to the Emotional Vibrations Tracking Chart).

To experience the Kingdom, do as Jesus instructed:

- Love God, love your neighbor (with today's shrinking world, this includes our neighbors from everywhere on the planet) as yourself, and love your enemies.

  Consider how you would solve problems—in your family and community, at the national level, or at the world level, if your solutions were made from Christ Consciousness.

- Love one another, for this will distinguish you as Disciples of Christ (or as being in Christ Consciousness).

- Forgive 70 times 7, for the grudge you hold is only harming *you*. The lower frequency of anger will cause disease in *your* body. (It has been said that a grudge is the poison you swallow, hoping the other person will die.).

- Clean up your own act rather than being concerned about the shortcomings of others. (Judge not the speck in your neighbor's eye; see the log in your own eye and attend to it first.)

- Show mercy and you will receive mercy. (What goes around comes around.)

- Blessed are the pure in heart, for they shall see God. (A pure heart is the one of loving kindness, acceptance, compassion, honoring, respect, and service with no strings attached.)

- Blessed are the peacemakers. (One person at the frequency level of 600 microwatts counteracts 10 million individuals who are below the level of 200 microwatts; imagine an army of peacemakers!)

- Archaic is the law of "an eye for an eye," which precipitates wars of the heart. From the vantage point of the 21st century, we can see what this kind of thinking has wrought over the ages.

- Live by the spirit of the law, not the letter of the law, as did the Pharisees. Do not let religious dogma rule you; know why a rule exists before you follow it blindly. As Paul said, "Test everything." (I Thes 5:21).

- You are the light of the world; let your Christ Consciousness shine brightly.

Do not worry about God wanting you to live a solemn life; it is not so. My personal knowledge from my experience of "sitting in the smile of God," indicates that the joy and love in store for us are beyond what most human beings can imagine, and supersedes any high of any sort that most people have ever experienced. We are in for a treat as we come into Christ Consciousness.

Let's go light up the world!

Tracking Your Accomplishments as a Light of the World

Write about your accomplishments in Section 4 of your journal.

CHAPTER 7

What Is Missing?

Dear Diary,

Today I feel a futility, a pointlessness to my life. I see myself and others living our lives with bitterness, in anger at the fact that we have no control. My whole life seems to be at the mercy of someone else or a circumstance beyond my control. What is the point of this? I want to make a difference, but I see that my mind is too small, my patterns too entrenched to make a different choice. I am doomed to a life of meaninglessness. How could I hope to fulfill some lofty great goal when I'm mired in hopelessness?

I think that it is a lie—the concept of a field of possibilities from which we may create the life of our dreams. I've bought into the lie, because for all my trying, I've only produced intense frustration and mistrust from the failed attempts to create a grand dream. I've only found that "same old same old" holds me in its grasp tightly. There's no co-creation of a bright future by design.

The Shift

Hmmmm. Now it occurs to me to ask: *What are my persistent thoughts and beliefs?* I like to think that I'm persistently positive. But look at these writings! I'm persistently depressed, distrusting, hopeless, and small-minded.

If it is my persistent thoughts that create from the field of possibilities, then no wonder I'm in trouble! I keep falling back into my old patterns of fear-based thinking.

How can I break through the pattern?

How can I once and for all shift my brain into persistently positive thinking??

Do I live my life so small because I don't have a greater vision for myself beyond the daily grind?

What if I did have a greater vision, would I live it?

What vision do I hold for my life?

Right now my vision is of a stuck place—between a rock and a hard place. I don't see myself beyond a struggle for survival. Work, pay the bills, and wish I didn't have to put up with idiots. I look for ways to numb out—TV, eating, shopping, gaming, Internet, a few beers or glasses of wine, smoking. This vision is not motivating enough to keep me going!

So, here I am—small, barely moving, miserable—asking: What shall I do? How can I end this?

I need a vision.

I need a means of fulfilling the vision: small steps to create it.

I need order to move out of chaos.

The vision sustains the reason to even bother to manage emotions. The vision gives hope and a purpose to be alive.

And so begins the joy of creating a vision.

Guided Imagery:

Using Metaphor of the Myth of the Flight of Daedalus and Icarus

You've been thrown into a prison. You may or may not know by whom, or why, and it doesn't matter. You do know that you've done your best, and you feel small and helpless against your circumstances. You look around and notice that you are trapped in a dark corner with nowhere to go. Your back is up against hard, cold stone. The cold from the stone floor permeates your feet and slithers up your spine, leaving you shivering and longing desperately for warmth. You are thinking: "What am I to do? How am I to escape?" In despair, you wail: "There is no way out!"

And then you notice it—a faint glow of light. In the darkness, you hadn't noticed that there is an open door that leads down a hall from which a barely visible light beckons. And yet here it is. Nothing stops you from taking a step forward, toward the glow of light, no matter how faint. Even though you are in pain, your curiosity is greater: What is that light? Where is it coming from? Is it warmer? Safer? So you take a step forward, and then another step. You find yourself leaving behind the densest darkness and stepping closer to the light, which reveals a bend in the hallway. The bend is quite some distance away. Discouragement surfaces, but the light beckons. Hope overcomes discouragement, and you continue. You are edging closer to an increasingly brighter ray of light. Around the bend, you see that the light is coming from a room with a window. Nothing is keeping you from going into the room and to the window.

Quickly now, you go to the window and peer out. You have a very high vantage point indeed. From the window, you see that your prison is actually a tower. From this tower, you have a high and wide view of your surroundings. The sky is a deep blue with small billowy clouds. The sun shines brightly. Birds are flying near and far. One bird is perched on a jutting stone near the window, singing its song as though it has no worries and neither should you. Your heart skips a beat. You think: "There is hope. Where there is light, there is hope!"

Then, looking down, you notice with dismay that you are at the very top of a high tower. You see that it is built on rocks at the edge of the sea. Great waves are crashing on the rocks below. "Sheesh" you say. "There's always something…"

You've found a larger space in which to dwell, and one with light and life, so there is improvement from where you found yourself not so long ago, but still, how are you to escape from this tower?

This time, however, your dismay is not as deep as the previous despair, for you put your situation in perspective. Not long ago, you were between a rock and a hard place, but now you are in a larger, lighter place. Before you were trapped, seemingly with no where to go, but then you noticed that there *was* somewhere to go, and with courage you took the necessary steps that brought you here.

There *is* forward movement.

That means that you can create further forward movement.

You pray, "Lord, show me what I must do next. I trust that there is a way. You've opened my eyes that I may see to come this far. I pray for strength and courage and further insight. I pray that my eyes remain open to see the way, and that my ears are attuned to hear what they must, and that the words I speak to create are only the powerful Truth."

Now, you see that your torturer is not totally heartless, for a door opens and a servant brings in a candle to stave off the dark of night. There is also a tray of food—a meager meal of bread and water and a scrap of meat that is mostly bone and gristle, but your hunger is not for food anyway. Your hunger is for a meaningful, bountiful life.

The bird that was chirping near the window now sits on the sill, still singing its song. You get an idea. It comes from the Greek myth of Daedalus and Icarus, wherein they escape their prison tower by making sets of wings and flying away. You see that you have all the materials they had for their great escape. And you have one thing they didn't—the insight from their mistake.

So you begin. With the bread, you lure the birds to the window, and while they eat, you harvest their feathers. Oh, yes, it takes ever so long, but this is your first step, and it *is* a step, which is better than nothing at all. From every meal you save the bread to lure the birds. As you harvest, you separate the feathers according to size. At long last you have enough feathers—it takes days, perhaps weeks, or if your imagination is particularly vivid, perhaps it takes merely hours—but the time it takes is not relevant. The work you do is. When you have enough feathers, you take a bone and fashion it into a needle. You unravel your shirt, using the threads to sew together rows of feathers. When all the feathers have been sewn together, you melt candle wax across the stitching to hold it all together firmly. Finally, you take the leather of your sandals to make straps to hold the wings onto your arms.

As in the myth, you spend days strapping on the wings, flapping to strengthen your arms in preparation for your flight.

The day comes when you are ready to fly. You remember the lesson from the story: you are to flap your wings at a steady pace. You are not to fly too low, where the dampness of the ocean can saturate your wings, making them too heavy to soar; nor are you to catch an updraft that spirals you up and up until you are too close to the sun, where heat will melt the wax of your wings, disintegrating them. No, you are to find that place that is just right, that sweet spot where your steady work is rewarded by a just-right uplifting current of air that takes you home.[10]

Making It Practical for Your Life

In your journal, turn to Section 7, "Small Vision."

For a few moments, rest within this ancient story. Allow it to bring to the surface your very own specific issues of pain and entrapment.

Now, consider what your "rock and a hard place" is. Write it down.

Is it possible there is a bend in your road of which you need only become aware?

Is it possible that just around the bend is something better?

How does that feel to think of that possibility? Write down your feelings.

Look up, look around. Be aware that there is a ray of light. Ask what that ray of light is. Name it.

---

10   A particularly fine version of this myth is Jane Yolen's *Wings.*

Be curious. If you walked toward the light, where might you find yourself?

Are you curious to know if it is a better place?

Are you willing to take the risk of leaving where you are, to see if it is a better place?

From there, might there be even more improvement?

You decide to take the first step toward the possibility of a better place. What is that first step?

Once you take the first step, is it not possible that the next step will become obvious? You don't need a great plan, only the *first* step, and faith in knowing that the next step will appear.

What resources might be available to you? Breadcrumbs, bird feathers, a bone-needle, the threads from your shirt, and candle wax are but metaphors. Your resources may be humble but they will provide the way out. Name your resources.

The key is steady progression toward the goal. The speed of your progression isn't the point. How can you keep steadily on task without dipping too low or soaring too high? As we learned from this myth, dipping or soaring can be dangerous and take us out of the game, or even end our life. Name how you are moving slowly but steadily toward improvement.

Write down in your journal any insights you received from this guided imagery.

CHAPTER 8

Having a Life Vision =
Joyful Living

L iving joyfully includes living one's life fully and living it in balance. To ensure that you are living fully and in balance, you must know what you want for your life. When you know what you want, you have a reason for getting up in the morning—a reason to do all that you do. Your reason for living as you do determines your degree of happiness.

Think about when you are happiest, when you feel fulfilled, how "time flies when you're having fun." Isn't life most joy-filled when you are doing what you love, being with the people whom you most appreciate, using your talents, enjoying the fruits of your labors, enjoying the environment that you have so thoughtfully created for yourself and your loved ones? This describes a life lived in the high-frequency spectrum of feelings.

Degrees of happiness coincide with the degree to which we realize our dreams. To realize your dream requires that you have a vision for your life, from creating the most awesome home environment for a happy family life, or building a career that makes your heart sing, or having fun with the children, the pets, or with friends, or making a difference in people's lives through service, to broadening your horizons through travel or education. Plugging into your dream of a rewarding life will bring you to fulfillment and joyful living.

Ask yourself, "Am I *fully* living my life, and living it in balance?"

In evaluating how full and balanced your life is, consider eight aspects of your life: your spiritual awareness, personal growth, relationships, physical environment, career, health, money, and fun and recreation. Each aspect needs high-frequency attention if life is to be full, rich, balanced, and joyful.

Let's look at each aspect individually. I've provided some questions to assist you with your evaluation. Answer the questions in Section 8 of your journal, "Life Vision."

Spiritual Awareness

- Do you have a daily spiritual practice such as taking time to pray, meditate, read sacred text, appreciate nature, or otherwise be inspired by the Divine?

- Describe your practice: Each day, how long do you devote to your practice? What does it consist of? Do you practice consistently?

- What is the result of this practice in your life?

- Describe how you feel the presence of God.

- What emotions and actions are expressed when you live from your Higher Self/"Christ Consciousness"?

- Describe the quality of your life as you live from Higher Self/"Christ Consciousness."

- Do you know yourself as a "creator"?

- Do you know yourself as an instrument through which The Divine/God/Higher Power may be expressed as light, love, and wisdom?

- Do you know your Oneness with The Divine/God/Higher Power?

Personal Growth

- What tools are in your "toolkit" for personal growth?

- What tools do you use most often?

- How have these tools made a difference in your life?

- How have you acquired these tools (e.g., church, sacred texts, workshops, classes, lectures, CDs, books, your own intuition, therapy, mentoring)?

- What life traumas have you overcome with the use of your tools?

- How far have you come in your personal growth since childhood?

- What is the greatest lesson you've learned from life?

- What wisdom have you gained that you would like to share?

- With whom would you like to share your wisdom?

- When will you share?

Relationships (with Self, Life Partner, Family, Friends, Employer, etc.)

Using these questions, describe your relationship with each family member and friend, starting with yourself:

- What works in the relationship?

- What do you like best about the relationship?

- How could you create even greater connection in the relationship?

- How could you create even greater happiness in the relationship?

- Describe any friction.

- If the friction recurs, is the reason usually the same?

- How could this issue be resolved on *your* part?

- Are you quick to forgive?

- What are the qualities of love?

- How do you express these qualities of love to each person in your life?

- Where and how could you do even better?

- What do you do together that creates happiness?

- What are the best qualities of your best friends?

- What do you contribute to the relationship?

- What does each person contribute to you?

- How do you support each other?

- How do you just have fun together?

- What do you need that you aren't getting?

- How can you get what you need?

- How do you reciprocate?

- Are your communications honest? Tactful? Kind?

- How could your communications be even better?

Physical Environment

- Describe your home (including the yard/garden):

  » What do you like best?

  » Do you have your own space?

  » Does your home and/or own space support your need for beauty? Function? Creativity? Fun? Love? Inspiration?

  » Is there room for improvement?

  » What are the ways that you can make it even better with what you have?

- Describe your office space using the same questions above.

- Describe you car using the same questions above.

Career

- What are all the things you like about your work?

- Are you doing what you love?

- Describe how it's fulfilling to you.

- How could it be even better?

- How do you affect others in your workplace?

- How do you affect others with the work you do?

Health

- In what ways do you enjoy your health?

- How do you maintain your health?

- How could you be even healthier?

- What will it take to be even healthier?

Money

- Describe your financial situation.

- If money were a person, how would you describe your relationship?

  » Do you respect money for what it can do for you?

  » Make a list of how money has made a contribution to your life.

  » What is your ongoing conversation with money? What do you say to it? What does it say to you?

  » Have you thanked money for the contribution it has made in your life?

  » Do you ever get the feeling that money (or perhaps the lack of it) controls your life?

  » How can you be the one in charge of money?

- Describe your money management techniques.

- Does your money work for you, or do you work for your money?

- How can you get your money working for you to create "passive income"?

- Who can help you with this?

- Describe how money can help you have an even better life.

- Describe how you make a difference in the world with your money.

- Would more money at your disposal allow you to make an even bigger difference? How?

Fun and Recreation

- What do you do for fun and recreation?

- How often?

- Do you allow yourself enough fun and recreation to feel relaxed and balanced?

- Is the quality of your fun in alignment with your values?

- Do you ever sabotage your fun?

- Do you have guilt when you are having fun? If so, describe it.

- How may you increase the quality of your fun and recreation?

Now that you've evaluated the quality of your life, you may want to rate each aspect on a scale of 0 to 10, with 10 being absolutely full and balanced. Write your rating in your journal next to each respective aspect.

You may wish to transfer your results from this exercise to the Wheel of Life graph on Page 87. This will give you a visual of a wheel representing the current smoothness or bumpiness of your ride through life.

Creating a Vision for Your Life

Now it's time to project five years into the future. Write a narrative in present tense about a typical day in your life five years from now, when you are living richly, fully, in balance and joy. Be as descriptive as possible, engaging each of the five senses. Do not forget to include what you are thankful for. Begin the narrative with you waking in the morning and end with you going to sleep at day's end. Include each of the eight aspects, either in an integrated narrative, or one by one.

Example (integrated):

It's time to get up. My honey and I cuddle before we begin our day, and never tire of time spent expressing our mutual love and admiration for each other.

We start our day with 60 minutes of spiritual practice: 30 minutes of meditating together, 10 minutes of Kirtan chanting, and 20 minutes of reading sacred text.

Next, we get dressed for our exercise routine, which is yoga, strength training, or a lovely brisk walk, depending on the day. I am so happy and grateful for being fit and healthy, as this keeps me able to live fully. I have strength and stamina to do all that I have and want to do. I am at my ideal weight of *** lbs.

After exercise, we prepare a healthy breakfast together. He loves to cook, by the way.

I am so happy and grateful for, and enthusiastic about, my work. I'm writing my fifth book. The other four have been fabulously successful in changing people's lives, and profitable for me in that my books have generated speaking engagements and high attendance at my workshops. I love my work. It fulfills my gifts and talents and desire to make a difference in the world.

We are planning another cruise with our kids and grandkids. This is a great way for the entire family to get together for pure, no-hassle fun. We do family cruises once a year to a different exotic place each time. He and I also have romantic get-aways, just the two of us.

We are planning a dinner party for friends on Saturday evening. This is one of our favorite activities. We have remarkable and eclectic friends who are all bright, talented, positive-thinking, thought-provoking, spiritual, supportive, and fun. Last week a bunch of us went to dinner and the symphony, and two weeks before that we and our rock'n'roll friends had a picnic at an outdoor rock concert. A jazz concert is coming up!

Affluence has made our lives so enjoyable, as well as allowing us to be major contributors to several charities, foundations, and causes that we believe in, and I am so happy and grateful that our tithe to our church is substantially supportive. With our annual income at $******, we are able to ensure our well-being and that of our family.

It's been a lovely day. It's dinner time. As with breakfast, we make the meal together. I love our large, spacious kitchen that has every amenity for creating a gourmet meal, although we more often prepare simple, highly nutritious meals. We create a romantic setting with candles in our lovely dining room. Our favorite music plays from our superb stereo system. Sometimes we eat out on the patio, with the waterfall gently splashing into the koi pond. The patio is where we often entertain, with the swimming pool just a few feet away. Our backyard is play-central for family and friends.

We love our home, which we have thoughtfully designed together to suit our needs for function and beauty. We both love art, which we have collected in our travels, and we have plenty of wall space and nooks and crannies to display it.

At day's end, we wind down by reading, watching, or listening to something inspirational. We meditate and pray together in gratitude for precious life and for healings wherever needed in our family, community, country, and the world. And then we go to bed for a good night's deep sleep.

I am so happy and grateful for my blessed life.

Your Life Vision

Now it is time for you to create your Life Vision. Write in your journal.

Figure 2 - Wheel of Life Exercise

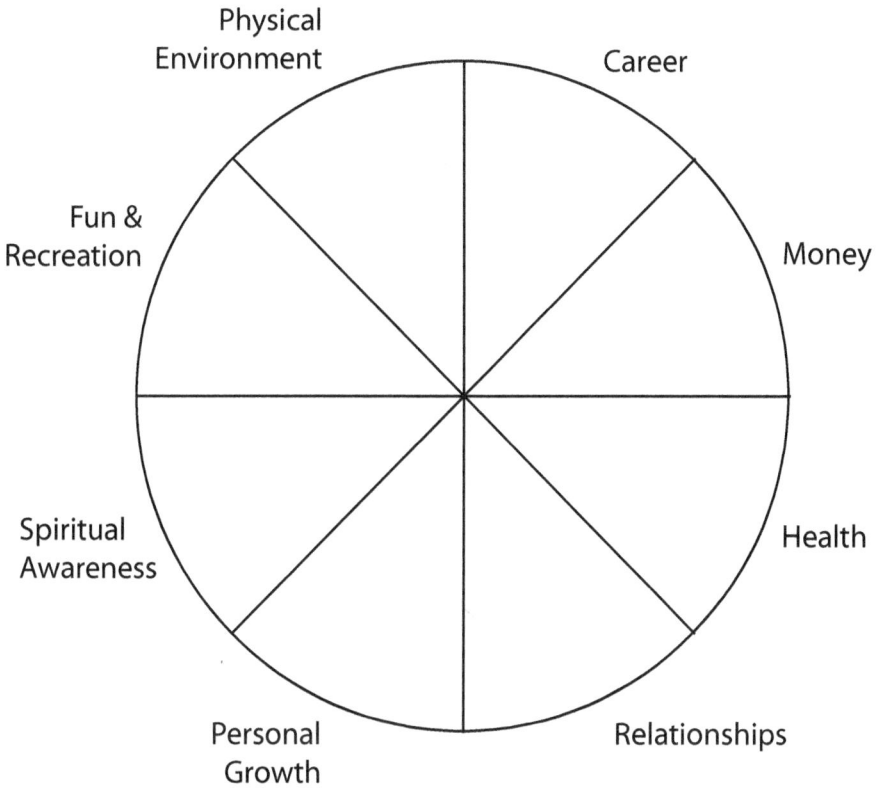

Directions: The eight sections in the Wheel of Life represent balance. Regarding the center of the wheel as 0 and the outer edge as 10, rank your level of satisfaction with each life area by drawing a straight or curved line to create a new outer edge (see example). The new perimeter of the circle represents your Wheel of Life. How bumpy would the ride be if this were a real wheel?

Example:

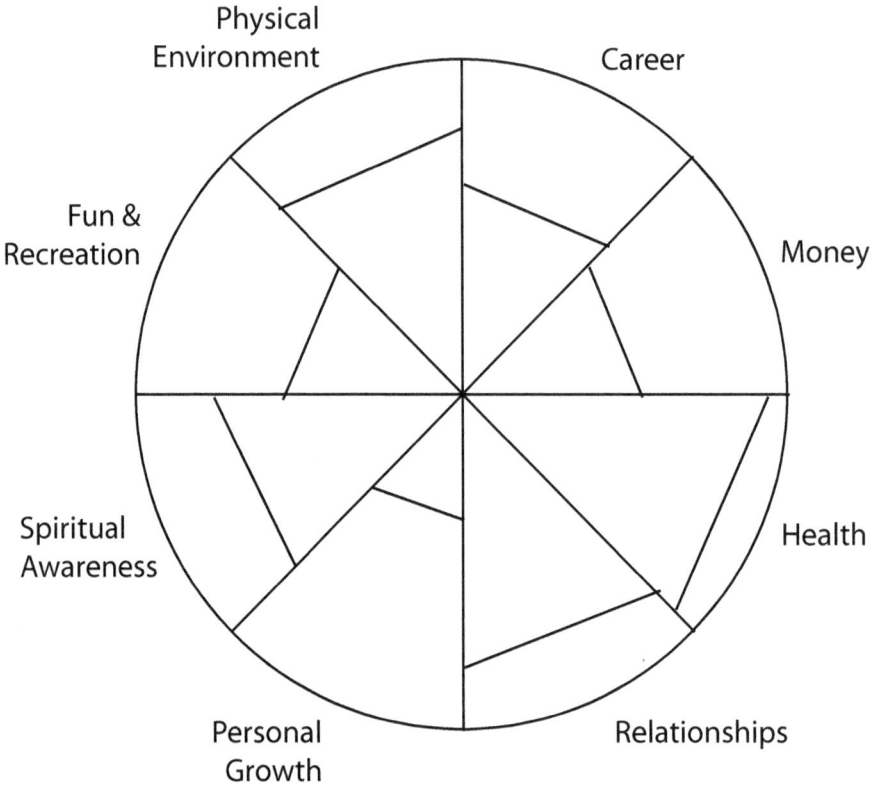

CHAPTER 9

Summary

If you have read to this page, then I know that you are interested in transforming your life.

If you have been following the guidelines as you have been reading, then I do not doubt that you are already experiencing shifts. I encourage you to keep doing the exercises, and to be cognizant of the changes occurring as you regularly review your journal. This will keep you aware of the progress you are making.

I invite you to be a light in the world, to be a "change agent" by first transforming yourself, and then by your example and by your increased vibration as you grow into your Christ Consciousness, you will positively influence others until together we will create heaven on earth, just as it is God's good pleasure for us.

The side effect of this is that you will be incomprehensibly happy. Your joy will be so great that you will wonder why you ever took so long to get going at creating your transformation.

Here is to your joyful journey, to praying constantly, and to giving thanks in all circumstances.

Namaste.

ABOUT THE AUTHOR

Sandra is a spiritual leader and counselor (as a Licensed Unity Teacher with the Assn of Unity Churches). She is a Mentor with a specialty in healing relationships with first oneself, God, other people (parents, spouse, children, boss, etc.), money, resources, and health. Sandra is an energy healer, working with the primary modalities of Reiki, Pranic Healing, and Psy-Chi Core Beliefs Healing.

ACKNOWLEDGEMENTS

Kudos to Donna Kozik, whose comprehensive service, Write a Book in a Weekend, finally got me doing what I've wanted to do since I was 9 years old—write a book and have it published. Her model for "getting 'er done" worked! And her guidance led me confidently through the entire process, from preparing to write, to writing, to publication, and even a strategy for marketing.

I am ever so grateful to friends Jim Westbury and Gail Nelson, who encouraged me and gave me honest, invaluable feedback on the first draft, and to Nina Love-Winslow for her feedback on the final draft.

Finally, at the end of the process, I am thankful to the Reverends Chris Chenoweth and Jim Peterson for their willingness to spend the time reading the manuscript and offering endorsements.

www.ingramcontent.com/pod-product-compliance
Lightning Source LLC
Chambersburg PA
CBHW071640050426
42443CB00026B/783